D0180369

# INTIMACY
## WITH
# GOD

### A DEVOTIONAL STUDY BY
## CYNTHIA HEALD

**NAVPRESS**

**BRINGING TRUTH TO LIFE**
NavPress Publishing Group
P.O.Box35001, Colorado Springs, Colorado 80935

The Navigators is an international Christian organization. Our mission is to reach, disciple, and equip people to know Christ and to make Him known through successive generations. We envision multitudes of diverse people in the United States and every other nation who have a passionate love for Christ, live a lifestyle of sharing Christ's love, and multiply spiritual laborers among those without Christ.

NavPress is the publishing ministry of The Navigators. NavPress publications help believers learn biblical truth and apply what they learn to their lives and ministries. Our mission is to stimulate spiritual formation among our readers.

(Originally published as *The Creator, My Confidant.*)

Cover illustration: Peter Pohle

Scripture quotations in this publication are from the *New American Standard Bible* (NASB)., © The Lockman Foundation 1960, 1962, 1963, 1968, 1971, 1972, 1973, 1975, 1977. Other versions used are: the *Holy Bible: New International Version* (NIV). Copyright © 1973, 1978, 1984, International Bible Society. Used by permission of Zondervan Bible Publishers; *The New English Bible* (NEB), © 1961, 1970 by the Delegates of the Oxford University Press and the Syndics of the Cambridge University Press; and *The Living Bible* © 1971. Used by permission of Tyndale House Publishers, Inc., Wheaton IL 60189. All rights reserved.

Printed in the United States of America

16 17 18 19 20 21 22 23 24 / 00 99 98 97

FOR A FREE CATALOG OF
NAVPRESS BOOKS & BIBLE STUDIES,
CALL 1-800-366-7788 (USA)
or 1-416-499-4615 (CANADA)

# Contents

## About the Author

Cynthia Hall Heald is a native Texan. She and her husband, Jack a veterinarian by profession, are on full-time staff with The Navigators in Tucson, Arizona. They have four children: Melinda, Daryl, Shelly, and Michael.

Cynthia graduated from the University of Texas with a B.A. in English. She speaks frequently to church women's groups and at seminars and retreats. Cynthia is also the author of *Becoming a Woman of Excellence, Becoming a Woman of Freedom, Becoming a Woman of Purpose,* and co-author of *Loving Your Wife.*

# Preface

The Lord had been prompting me to study the psalms. To reinforce His desire, He prompted a friend to give me *The Treasury of David*. C. H. Spurgeon, who edited this treasury, wrote, "More and more is the conviction forced upon my heart that every man must traverse the territory of the Psalms himself if he would know what a goodly land they are. They flow with milk and honey, but not to strangers; they are only fertile to lovers of their hills and vales. None but the Holy Spirit can give a man the key to the Treasury of David; and even He gives it rather to experience than to study. Happy he who for himself knows the secret of the Psalms." A little reluctantly, I began my pilgrimage into this vast poetical land. For two years, I have listened to, cried with, and learned from these special men of God. I am no longer a stranger, but now I desire to take up a long-term residence in these hills and vales.

How much the psalmists have taught me about relating to and being intimate with God. My heart is humbled deep within me, for I have realized how shallow my concept of walking with God has been. Still, I am deeply encouraged, for the psalmists have shown me not only their heart's response in all situations, but they have also meaningfully testified to God's heart in faithfully relating to them in those situations. Because of this study, I dare call the Creator my intimate Friend.

CYNTHIA HEALD

## Part One
## **The Desire for Intimacy**

### Our Longing for Intimacy
### God's Desire for Us

In the beginning, Adam and Eve enjoyed a very special, deep, intimate relationship with God and with each other. "The man and his wife were both naked," we are told, but they were "not ashamed." Their nakedness symbolized their freedom and confidence in God's love for them and their acceptance of and trust in each other.

After the tragic intrusion of Satan and his deception, Adam and Eve hid themselves from the presence of the Lord. Their close fellowship with God was irrevocably broken. Dan Allender writes that Adam's nakedness referred to "his awareness of being utterly exposed as helpless and contemptible" (I.B.C. Perspective, 1985, Vol. I, No. 1). Adam himself told God, "I heard the sound of Thee in the garden, and I was afraid because I was naked; so I hid myself."

As it was in the beginning; so it is now. We find ourselves still tenuous in our relating to God—hiding, yet answering

Him when He calls, "Where are you?" Dare we move away from among the trees? Despite our fear and shame, we sense our need not only for reconciliation, but also for restoration to that original, intimate relationship with our heavenly Father. We know that within each of us is a God-shaped vacuum that only He can fill.

Just as God provided garments of skin for Adam and Eve, so He has provided for us a Savior, Christ the Lord. When we accept Him, He clothes us in His righteousness so that we can draw near with confidence to the throne of grace. In Christ, we are secure and free in our standing before God. We can step out from whatever trees of fear we may feel surround us ("His perfect love casts out fear"). We are no longer bound by the belief that if we really tell God how we feel or what we think we will be judged or God will cause some disaster to come upon us.

This is true intimacy: being confident that what we reveal about ourselves will be understood and that the person with whom we disclose ourselves will accept us, seek our good, and communicate support and love.

But practically, how do we deepen our friendship with God? Who has gone before us to show us the way? It is the psalmists, who, in their honesty, vulnerability, and revelations of the heart, demonstrate to us how to relate to God intimately. It is in studying and meditating on the psalms that we find courage to expose our hearts to our Creator and learn to say confidently, "The Lord is *my* Shepherd, I shall not want."

# CHAPTER ONE
## Our Longing for Intimacy

---◆---

Whom have I in heaven but thee?
And having Thee, I desire nothing else on earth.
(Psalm 73:25, NEB)

◆

Can we find a friend so faithful,
Who will all our sorrows share?
Jesus knows our every weakness—
Take it to the Lord in prayer.[1]

◆

Come near to the holy men and women of the past and you
will soon feel the heat of their desire after God.
They mourned for Him, they prayed and wrestled and
sought for Him day and night, in season and out,
and when they had found Him the finding was all the
sweeter for the long seeking.[2]
(A.W. Tozer)

| Needs or circumstances that prompted the psalmist's prayer | Key words or phrases that express the psalmist's need for intimacy | vv. |
|---|---|---|
| Psalm 42 | | |
| Psalm 63 | | |
| Psalm 73 | | |
| Psalm 86 | | |
| Psalm 88 | | |

# Our Longing for Intimacy

There is a restlessness deep within each of us that compels us to search for the person, the place, the job, the "god" that will fill the void and give us peace. This restlessness essentially becomes a pursuit to find someone who will love us for who we are, understand our fears and anxieties, affirm our worth, and call our lives into account. To admit our need and dependence upon God requires humility and vulnerability, which paves the way not only for knowing God, but also for becoming intimate with Him. "Mutual love and confidence are the keys to intimacy," writes J. O. Sanders, "deepening intimacy with God is the outcome of *deep desire.*"[3]

May the prayer of David be our prayer:

> Hear my cry, O God;
> Give heed to my prayer.
> From the end of the earth
>     I call to Thee, when my heart is faint;
> Lead me to the rock that is higher than I.
> For Thou hast been a refuge for me,
> A tower of strength against the enemy.
> Let me dwell in Thy tent forever;
> Let me take refuge in the shelter of Thy wings.
>
>                           Psalm 61:1-4

## Observation

1. The preceding psalms (see chart on page 10) are particularly rich in communicating man's desire for closeness with God. Read through each one carefully, and then go back to them a second time to make two observations: (1) the need or circumstances that seemed to have prompted the psalmist's prayer, and (2) the key words or phrases used by the psalmist to express his need for intimacy. Write down the corresponding verse references in the far right column.

---

Such as are most heartily afflicted in spirit, and do flee to God for reconciliation and consolation through Christ, have no reason to suspect themselves, that they are not esteemed of and loved as dear children, because they feel so much of God's wrath: for here is a saint who hath drunken of that cup (as deep as any who shall read this Psalm), here is one so much loved and honored of God, as to be a pensmen of Holy Scripture, and a pattern of faith and patience unto others; even Hemen the Ezrahite.[4]

David Dickson

---

2. Choose one or two circumstances mentioned in the psalms you just read and explore the possible reasons why these situations prompted the psalmist's desire for intimacy with God. To help guide your thinking, ask yourself, "Why is it that a situation such as this would cause a man or woman to feel the need to draw close to God?"

3. What evidences can you find of the psalmist's knowledge and experience of God—that is, what is the psalmist's view of God? (You may prefer to select just one or two psalms to answer this question.)

4. Why do you think the psalmist sought God, and God only, to meet his needs? What other sources might he have drawn upon to meet his needs?

If we have a godly thirst, it will appear by diligence in frequenting the place and means of grace; brute beasts for want of water will break through hedges, and grace-thirsty souls will make their ways through all encumbrances to come where they may have satisfaction.[5]

Thomas Pierson

### Expression

Paul wrote to Timothy, "At my first defense no one supported me, but all deserted me. . . . But the Lord stood with me, and strengthened me" (2 Timothy 4:16-17). As with Paul, so it is with us. There is really only One we can rely on with the confidence that we will never be forsaken. So I am drawn to His faithfulness and love for me. The more I admit my need for intimacy with the Lord, the more I desire Him; the more I desire Him, the deeper my intimacy.

5. Select one passage revealing the psalmist's desire for God that especially stood out to you. Write it down here, as well as why it is significant to you. If you wish, write out your reason for its significance in the form of a short prayer or psalm, expressing your feelings about drawing closer to God.

Great as He is He loves His children to be bold with Him.[6]

C. H. Spurgeon

The psalms are not the only Scriptures that speak of intimacy. In the future as you read through other portions of the Bible, you might want to note favorite passages that convey the same thoughts as the psalmists in a particular subject area. This could give you a good beginning to a topical study.

**Other Scriptures:** Isaiah 26:9, Philippians 3:7-11

**Notes**
1. From the hymn "What a Friend We Have in Jesus," by Joseph M. Scriven and Charles C. Converse.
2. A. W. Tozer, *The Pursuit of God* (Harrisburg, PA: Christian Publications, n.d.), p. 15.
3. J. Oswald Sanders, *Enjoying Intimacy with God* (Chicago: Moody Press, 1980), p. 20.
4. David Dickson, in *The Treasury of David*, by C. H. Spurgeon, Vol. II (McLean, VA: MacDonald Publishing Co., n.d.), p. 8.
5. Thomas Pierson, in *The Treasury of David*, by Spurgeon, Vol. II, p. 343.
6. Charles Haddon Spurgeon, *The Treasury of David*, Vol. II, p. 463.

## CHAPTER TWO
## God's Desire for Us

◆

When Thou didst say, "Seek My face," my heart said to Thee,
"Thy face, O LORD, I shall seek."
(Psalm 27:8)

◆

There's the wonder of sunset at evening,
The wonder as sunrise I see;
But the wonder of wonders that thrills my soul
Is the wonder that God loves me.[1]

◆

What matters supremely, therefore, is not,
in the last analysis, the fact that I know God, but the larger
fact which underlies it—the fact that He knows me. I am
graven on the palms of His hands; I am never out of His
mind. All my knowledge of Him depends on His sustained
initiative in knowing me. I know Him because He first knew
me and continues to know me.[2]
(J. I. Packer)

| God's desire | David's response | vv. |
|---|---|---|
| Psalm 8 | | |
| Psalm 23 | | |
| Psalm 33 | | |
| Psalm 139 | | |

# God's Desire for Us

"Amazing love! How can it be, that Thou, my God, shouldst die for me!" This great hymn by Charles Wesley conveys the wonder of God's desire to have fellowship with us. The God who created us has not abandoned us to grope blindly through life. He has provided, at great expense, all that we need for life and godliness. God is our *personal* Creator, and He wants to be our Shepherd who protects and provides for us. He has proclaimed His love for us, and He waits only for our response.

> Many, O LORD my God, are the wonders which Thou has done,
> And Thy thoughts toward us;
> There is none to compare with Thee;
> If I would declare and speak of them,
> They would be too numerous to count.
>
> Psalm 40:5

## Observation

1. God's desire for us is uniquely expressed in the psalms listed on the previous page (see chart on page 16). After reading through these psalms, write down the key thoughts and phrases that convey God's desire for us and David's response to God's care.

———◆———

Concerning Psalm 23 Charles Spurgeon writes: "The sweetest word of the whole is that monosyllable, 'MY.' He does not say, 'The Lord is the shepherd of the world at large, and leadeth forth the multitude of the flock,' but, 'The Lord is *my* shepherd.'"[3]

———◆———

## Reflection

2. In the psalms you just read through, what specific assur-

17

ances does the psalmist express about God's involvement in his emotions and experiences?

3. What do these observations about God's activity tell us about His nature and character?

4. What do David's responses reveal about his concept of God?

If, then, you feel not your soul mightily affected with the condescension of God, say thus unto your souls, "What aileth thee, O my soul, that thou are no more affected with the goodness of God?... Oh the condescension of his love, to visit me, to sue unto me, to wait upon me, to be acquainted with me?"[4]

### Expression

It wasn't until I was a parent that I began to realize God's desire to be intimate with His children. Spiritually I was born into God's family, just as my children were physically born into our family. But it is not enough just to bear children; there is a great desire on the part of a parent to have a vital relationship, a bond of intimacy with his or her child. In a small way, I understand God's desire to be lovingly involved and close to us, just as I love and want to be near my children.

5. a. Write out one passage that is most significant to you in expressing the nature of God's desire for us. (You might want to memorize it this week.)

  b. What kind of response would you most like to offer to this revelation of who God is? (If you like, express your thoughts in the form of a psalm or prayer.)

---◆---

God's omniscience is one of the most comforting truths I know, because it means that He knows the core of my wicked heart and chooses to remain in relationship with His imperfect servant.[5]

Dan Allender

---◆---

**Other Scriptures:** Jeremiah 24:7, Matthew 11:25-30, Revelation 21:2-4

**Notes**
1. From the hymn "The Wonder of It All," by George Beverly Shea.
2. J. I. Packer, *Knowing God* (Downers Grove, IL: InterVarsity Press, 1979), p. 37.
3. Spurgeon, *The Treasury of David*, Vol. I, p. 354.
4. Janeway, in *The Treasury of David*, by Spurgeon, Vol. I, p. 89.
5. Dan Allender, in *IBC Perspective: A Publication of the Institute of Biblical Counseling*, ed. Lawrence J. Crabb, Jr. (Winona Lake, IN, 1985), Vol. I, No. 1, p. 27.

19

## Part Two
## The Creator, a Worthy Confidant

### God Is Righteous
### God Is Trustworthy
### God Is a Refuge
### God Is Responsive

◆

Intimacy connotes familiarity and closeness. It involves our deepest nature, and is marked by a warm friendship developed through long association. In order for us to become intimate with another, we must find in him a true confidant— one to whom we can safely confide our secrets.

What are the characteristics of such a true friend? Most of us look for someone we respect as wise and just, who we can trust implicitly, with whom we feel safe and secure, and who will respond to us, help us in the right way, and be available whenever we want to share. True confidants are rare, and fortunate are those who have one.

There is One who meets these criteria perfectly: the Keeper of souls who never sleeps, who has called us into fellowship with His Son, Jesus Christ our Lord, and who continually bids us to "Call to Me, and I will answer you, and I will tell you great and mighty things, which you do not know." Realizing that God is that worthy confidant is necessary to our becoming intimate with Him. The psalmists affirm to us that the Creator can become our confidant.

## CHAPTER THREE
## God Is Righteous

◆

Righteousness and justice are the foundation of Thy throne;
Lovingkindness and truth go before Thee.
How blessed are the people who know the joyful sound!
O LORD, they walk in the light of Thy countenance.
(Psalm 89:14-15)

◆

My hope is built on nothing less
Than Jesus' blood and righteousness;
I dare not trust the sweetest frame,
But wholly lean on Jesus' name.[1]

◆

Our Father, we love Thee for Thy justice. We acknowledge
that Thy judgments are true and righteous altogether.
Thy justice upholds the order of the universe and guarantees
the safety of all who put their trust in Thee.
We live because Thou art just—and merciful. Holy, holy,
holy, Lord God Almighty, righteous in all Thy ways
and holy in all Thy works. Amen.[2]
(A. W. Tozer)

| Declarations or evidences of God's righteous character | vv. |
|---|---|
| Psalm 9 | |
| Psalm 71 | |
| Psalm 78 | |
| Psalm 103 | |

# God Is Righteous

It is a comforting thought to know that God is righteous. Righteous essentially means meeting the standards of what is right and just. Righteousness involves goodness, uprightness, integrity, morality, and purity. Righteous means right! Sinclair Ferguson expounds further by asking the question: "But what is the righteousness of God? The idea behind the biblical word *righteousness* is probably 'conformity to a norm.' Given that norm, righteousness is the situation in which things are what they ought to be. In the Old Testament, righteousness is associated with God's covenant. He is faithful to it; in relation to His promise, God always does what He ought to do, namely, fulfill His promise. That is why His righteousness can be expressed in judgment, or in salvation."[3]

> But as for me, I will hope continually,
> And will praise Thee yet more and more.
> My mouth shall tell of Thy righteousness,
> And of Thy salvation all day long;
> For I do not know the sum of them.
> I will come with the mighty deeds of the Lord GOD;
> I will make mention of Thy righteousness, Thine alone.
>
> Psalm 71:14-16

## Observation

1. In this group of psalms (see chart on page 24), look for declarations or evidences of God's righteous character in dealing with His people's obedience or sinfulness.

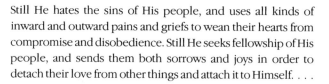

> Still He hates the sins of His people, and uses all kinds of inward and outward pains and griefs to wean their hearts from compromise and disobedience. Still He seeks fellowship of His people, and sends them both sorrows and joys in order to detach their love from other things and attach it to Himself. . . .

So we read of Him dealing with His people in the Scripture record, and so He deals with them still. His aims and principles of action remain consistent; He does not at any time act out of character. Man's ways, we know, are pathetically inconstant—but not God's.[4]

J. I. Packer

## Reflection

2. Choose one or two declarations or evidences of God's righteous character. What were the experiences that enabled the psalmists to reach this understanding of God's righteous character?

3. Notice the psalmist's technique of recounting history in Psalm 78. Why do you think it was necessary for the psalmist to review God's past action in the lives of His people?

4. How did the psalmist's comprehension of God's righteousness impact his life? Look for specific evidences of how this understanding made a difference.

———————◆———————

We survive in the way of faith not because we have extraordinary stamina but because God is righteous. Christian discipleship is a process of paying more and more attention to God's righteousness and less and less attention to our own; finding the meaning of our lives not by probing our moods and motives and morals but by believing in God's will and purposes; making a map of the faithfulness of God, not charting the rise and fall of our enthusiasms. It is out of such a reality that we acquire perseverance.[5]

Eugene Peterson

———————◆———————

## Expression

When I come to God and I am hurt, confused, or angry, I know that no matter what I say God will judge righteously. I cannot persuade God to justify me if I am to blame in any way. This gives me great freedom to confide in Him. He sifts through my feelings and "causes" and either confronts or consoles me in righteousness and justice.

5. Which declaration or evidence of God's righteousness means the most to you? Why?

———————◆———————

Let the words of my mouth—what I say—and the meditation of my heart—what I think—be the kind of words and thoughts that have sat under the judgment of your work, Father, reflecting the instruction, the light and the love of your heart, so that what I am, both inside and outside, will be acceptable before you.[6]

Ray Stedman

———————◆———————

**Other Scriptures:** Nehemiah 9:7-8, 2 Thessalonians 1:5-8

**Notes**
1. From the hymn "The Solid Rock," by Edward Mote and William B. Bradbury.
2. A. W. Tozer, *The Knowledge of the Holy* (New York: Harper & Row, 1961), p. 92.
3. Sinclair Ferguson, *Kingdom Life in a Fallen World* (Colorado Springs, CO: NavPress, 1986), pp. 45-46.
4. Packer, *Knowing God,* p. 71.
5. Eugene Peterson, *A Long Obedience in the Same Direction* (Downers Grove, IL: InterVarsity Press, 1980), pp. 128-129.
6. Ray Stedman, *Folk Songs of Faith,* from the *Bible Commentary for Laymen* series (Glendale, CA: Gospel Light Publications, 1973), p. 47.

## CHAPTER FOUR
## God Is Trustworthy

————————◆————————

In Thee our fathers trusted;
They trusted, and Thou didst deliver them.
To Thee they cried out, and were delivered;
In Thee they trusted, and were not disappointed.
(Psalm 22:4-5)

◆

'Tis so sweet to trust in Jesus,
Just to take Him at His word,
Just to rest upon His promise,
Just to know, "Thus saith the Lord."[1]

◆

Be assured, if you walk with Him and look to Him and
expect help from Him, He will never fail you. As an older
brother who has known the Lord for forty-four years,
who writes this, says to you for your encouragement that He
has never failed him. In the greatest difficulties, in the
heaviest trials, in the deepest poverty and necessities, He has
never failed me; but because I was enabled by His grace to
trust Him He has always appeared for my help. I delight in
speaking well of His name.[2]
(George Mueller)

| Circumstances that prompted the psalmist to trust in God | vv. |
|---|---|
| Psalm 31 | |
| Psalm 37 | |
| Psalm 40 | |
| Psalm 56 | |
| Psalm 84 | |

# God Is Trustworthy

The young girl sitting across from me cried softly, "I'm afraid that if I trust God, I'll experience some cosmic disillusionment." How can we confidently believe that God is reliable, dependable, and committed to our care? How do we know that if we give Him our lives and reveal to Him our deepest desires, some tragedy will not befall us?

The psalmists who have gone before us can help answer our questions. So much depends on our knowing God's character, understanding His performance in the past, and seeing life from His viewpoint. In Psalm 84:11 we read, "No good thing does He withhold from those who walk uprightly." Sir Richard Baker comments, "But how is this true, when God oftentimes withholds riches and honours and health of body from men, though they walk ever so uprightly; we may therefore know that honours and riches and bodily strength are none of God's good things; . . . the good things of God are chiefly peace of conscience and joy in the Holy Ghost in this life; fruition of God's presence, and vision of his blessed face in the next, and these good things God never bestows upon the wicked, and never withholds from the godly."[3]

Trust would not be trust if it did not require some commitment from us to walk by faith and not by sight. God is a trustworthy confidant, for He constantly seeks our good.

> Blessed be the LORD,
> Because He has heard the voice of my supplication.
> The LORD is my strength and my shield;
> My heart trusts in Him, and I am helped;
> Therefore my heart exults,
> And with my song I shall thank Him.
>
> Psalm 28:6-7

## Observation
1. An abiding trust in God is the theme of the psalms in this

chapter. Read through each one, and record the circumstances that prompted the psalmist to trust in God (use the chart on page 30).

———————◆———————

Charles Spurgeon sheds light on Psalm 56:3 by commenting that fear can draw us closer to God: "It is a blessed fear which drives us to trust. Unregenerate fear drives from God, gracious fear drives to Him. If I fear man I have only to trust God, and I have the best antidote. To trust when there is no cause for fear, is but the name of faith, but to be reliant upon God when occasions for alarm are abundant and pressing, is the conquering faith of God's elect. Though the verse is in the form of a resolve, it became a fact in David's life, let us make it so in ours. Whether the fear arise from without or within, from past, present, or future, from temporals or spirituals, from men or devils, let us maintain faith, and we shall soon recover courage."[4]

———————◆———————

### Reflection

2. List the various circumstances that prompted the psalmists to put their trust in God.

3. Summarize the main reasons the psalmists stated for trusting God.

4. What other aspects of the psalmist's life were touched because of his trust in God?

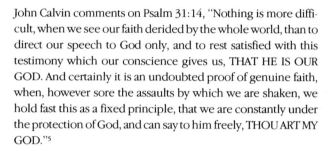

John Calvin comments on Psalm 31:14, "Nothing is more diffi-cult, when we see our faith derided by the whole world, than to direct our speech to God only, and to rest satisfied with this testimony which our conscience gives us, THAT HE IS OUR GOD. And certainly it is an undoubted proof of genuine faith, when, however sore the assaults by which we are shaken, we hold fast this as a fixed principle, that we are constantly under the protection of God, and can say to him freely, THOU ART MY GOD."[5]

### Expression

Our oldest daughter was scheduled to have a tumor removed from her pituitary. She made the following observation: "I am not afraid to have this surgery. I have talked with the doctor and I am very confident of his ability, and I really trust him." She then added: "I wonder why we struggle so with trusting God with our lives?"

5. Choose one of the psalmists' reasons for trusting God that particularly challenged you. Express to God why this rea-son is important to you, in the form of a short paragraph, prayer, or psalm.

---

It is as if God were saying, "What I am is all that need matter to you, for there lie your hope and your peace. I will do what I will do, and it will all come to light at last, but how I do it is My secret. Trust Me, and be not afraid."[6]

A. W. Tozer

---

**Other Scriptures:** Isaiah 26:4, Jeremiah 17:5-8, 1 Timothy 4:9-10

**Notes**
1. From the hymn "'Tis So Sweet to Trust in Jesus," by Louisa M. R. Stead and William J. Kirkpatrick.
2. George Mueller, in *Streams in the Desert*, compiled by Mrs. Charles E. Cowman (Minneapolis, MN: Worldwide Publications, 1979), pp. 19-20.
3. Sir Richard Baker, in *The Treasury of David*, by Spurgeon, Vol. II, p. 446.
4. Spurgeon, *The Treasury of David*, Vol. I, p. 465.
5. John Calvin, in *The Treasury of David*, by Spurgeon, Vol. I, part 2, p. 72.
6. Tozer, *The Knowledge of the Holy*, p. 70.

## CHAPTER FIVE
## God Is a Refuge

I cried out to Thee, O LORD;
I said, "Thou art my refuge,
My portion in the land of the living."
(Psalm 142:5)

♦

How often in conflict, when pressed by the foe,
I have fled to my Refuge and breathed out my woe;
How often, when trials like sea-billows roll,
Have I hidden in Thee, O Thou Rock of my soul.[1]

♦

He is both *shelter*, offering protection, and *shadow*, offering
refreshment; He offers not only a dwelling-place, but, as the
verb *abides* [Psalm 91:1] indicates, makes Himself our Host
and makes us His protected guests, safe because it is His
duty to make us safe.[2]

| Words or phrases describing God as a refuge | vv. |
|---|---|
| Psalm 18 | |
| Psalm 46 | |
| Psalm 62 | |
| Psalm 91 | |

# God Is a Refuge

A refuge provides protection or shelter from danger or hardship. It is a haven or sanctuary, a place where one may go for help, relief, or escape. Who among us does not seek a secure refuge from the daily harassments and stresses of life? There are many false refuges: the over-involvement in recreation or hobbies, the hiding of oneself in work activities, the single-minded pursuit of acquiring possessions, and the losing of self in drug-dependency. These are some major ways that we, as a society, seek comfort. But there is only one refuge that offers personal, eternal protection and provision. "There is a place of quiet rest, near to the heart of God."

> For my eyes are toward Thee, O GOD, the Lord;
> In Thee I take refuge; do not leave me defenseless.
> Psalm 141:8

## Observation

1. The psalmists who penned these "refuge" psalms (listed in chart on page 36) vividly express their confidence in God's protection. Record the words or phrases they use to describe God as a refuge.

——————◆——————

Psalm 46:7: The naming of God is done here with great care. LORD OF HOSTS paints a picture: "hosts" are "armies"—vast, angelic troops, swift and fell, carrying out the divine command. GOD OF JACOB recalls a story: the persistent assailant at the river Jabbok who wrestled Jacob into the intimacy of blessing. A powerful God, "LORD of hosts," and a personal God, "God of Jacob." But there is a surprising reversal in the way these names are connected with our expectations. We expect the military metaphor to be associated with defense, "refuge." We expect the personal metaphor to be connected with intimacy, "with us." But the terms are deliberately rearranged so that we get

37

intimacy with the warrior God and defense from the family friend. A powerful God (LORD of hosts) befriends (is with us); a personal God (God of Jacob) protects (is our refuge).[3]

Eugene Peterson

---◆---

## Reflection

2. Look back at the psalmists' descriptions of God as a refuge in Psalms 18 and 91. What circumstances occurred in the psalmists' lives that led them to seek God's protection?

3. a. What hindrances for making God a refuge are found in Psalm 52?

b. Why do you think these things would keep us from finding shelter in God?

4. What results or benefits are cited by the psalmists because they had sought God as a refuge?

---◆---

To take up a general truth and make it our own by personal faith is the highest wisdom. It is but poor comfort to say "the Lord is a refuge"; but to say He is MY refuge, is the essence of consolation.[4]

C. H. Spurgeon

---◆---

### Expression

As a child, playing the game of hide and seek, I always felt excited and secure whenever I found a safe hiding place. As a grown-up, I still tend to look for places where I can hide! The problem with life, though, is that I cannot just disappear whenever I wish. How encouraging it is to know that in the midst of turmoil, my spirit can seek the Hiding Place and be secure in the knowledge that my life is hidden with Christ in God, our true refuge.

5. a. Look back at your observation in question 1 of the images used to describe God as a refuge. What do you think those images communicated to the psalmists about God's nature and character?

b. If you were a psalmist writing today, what images would you choose to portray God as a refuge?

HIS THOUGHTS SAID: Before me continually is the grief of wounds, confusion, suspense, distress. HIS FATHER SAID: Behold, there is a place by ME, and thou shalt stand upon a rock. Then as a frightened child on a storm-swept mountainside would gratefully take his father's hand, and stand on a rock in a place by him, fearing no evil—so it was with the son. For he knew that though the earth be removed and the waters be carried into the midst of the sea, that rock by his Father would never be moved.[5]

Amy Carmichael

**Other Scriptures:** Deuteronomy 33:27, Hebrews 6:13-20

**Notes**
1. From the hymn "Hiding in Thee," by William O. Cushing and Ira D. Sankey.
2. *The New Bible Commentary*, ed. Donald Guthrie (Grand Rapids, MI: Wm. B. Eerdmans Publishing Co.), p. 508.
3. Eugene Peterson, *Earth and Altar* (Downers Grove, IL: InterVarsity Press, 1985), pp. 72-73.
4. Spurgeon, *The Treasury of David*, Vol. II, Psalm 91:2, p. 89.
5. Amy Carmichael, *His Thoughts Said . . . His Father Said . . .* (Ft. Washington, PA: Christian Literature Crusade, 1941), #113.

## CHAPTER SIX
## God Is Responsive

◆

I love the LORD, because He hears
My voice and my supplications.
Because He has inclined His ear to me,
Therefore I shall call upon Him as long as I live.
(Psalm 116:1-2)

◆

And Jesus said, "Come to the water, stand by my side;
I know you are thirsty, you won't be denied.
I felt every teardrop when in darkness you cried,
And I strove to remind you that for those tears I died."[1]

◆

God is personal so that we may have an intimate
relationship with him; God is redeemer so that
we may be helped by him.[2]
(Eugene Peterson)

| Situations that prompted calls for God's help | vv. |
|---|---|
| Psalm 32 | |
| Psalm 107 | |
| Psalm 116 | |
| Psalm 145 | |

# God Is Responsive

There are counselors who listen to people bare their anguished souls, and then respond by either nodding their heads or asking, "Well, what do you think should be done?" Their counselees eventually leave feeling very frustrated and hopeless.

Not so with God as our confidant. As we learn from this next group of psalms, when the redeemed cry for help, He responds and rescues.

We will also study in this chapter circumstances of our own making that may prevent God from responding. A popular saying raises the question, "If God seems far away, guess who moved?"

God delights in showing Himself mighty on our behalf. What a privilege to call upon Him and "consider the loving-kindness of the LORD."

> On the day I called Thou didst answer me;
> Thou didst make me bold with strength in my soul.
> Psalm 138:3

## Observation
1. a. The writers of the psalms (see page 42) proclaim God's goodness in responding to them. List the situations that seemed to have prompted their calls for God's help.

   b. In the following passages, record the hindrances that would keep God from responding.

   Psalm 5:4-6

43

Psalm 53:1-3

Psalm 66:18

Psalm 73:21-22

Psalm 81:11-16

## Reflection

2. Choose several ways God responded to the psalmists' cries for help that were meaningful to you. How did God respond, and why do these responses seem significant to you?

3. Summarize the criteria you can find that are necessary for God's responding.

4. There are times in our lives when God seems unresponsive. Psalm 88, which we looked at in chapter 1 as an expression of longing for God, is a good example of such troubling times.

    What insights have you gained from this chapter that would help when God seems to be silent?

---◆---

Aptly, but dreadfully, the last word of the psalm [88] is *darkness,* and yet therein lies its wonder—the wonder of triumphant faith, that a man should see no light at all but yet go on supplicating in fervent, trustful, ceaseless prayer. . . . What is to be done when the promises of God are denied by the facts of experience? . . . Turn the promises into prayers and plead them before God.[3]

---◆---

5. What seem to be the key lessons about God's responding to us that can be learned from the psalms you've just studied in this chapter?

---◆---

"And he saved them out of their distresses." Speedily and willingly He sent relief. They were long before they cried, but He was not long before He saved. They had applied everywhere else before they came to Him, but when they did address themselves to Him, they were welcome at once. He who saved men in the open wilderness can also save in the closed prison: bolts and bars cannot shut Him out, nor long shut in His redeemed ones.[4]

C. H. Spurgeon

---◆---

**Expression**

It is hard for me to realize that God is responsive, or that He intervenes on my behalf. There seems to be something deep down inside of me that lingers in my thoughts: I'm not really sure He'll respond. I need to remember that "no" and "wait" are just as valid answers as "yes." Perhaps, though, the majority of my problem is not in believing that God will respond, it's fearing that He won't answer when and how I want Him to!

6. Look back at the list of hindrances in the "Observation" section of this study chapter. How does this list help you in

46

understanding God's character, His responsiveness, and the basis of our intimacy with Him?

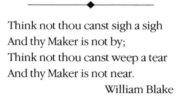

Think not thou canst sigh a sigh
And thy Maker is not by;
Think not thou canst weep a tear
And thy Maker is not near.

William Blake

**Other Scriptures:** Jeremiah 33:3, James 4:8

**Notes**

1. From the hymn "For Those Tears I Died," by Marsha Stevens, © Copyright 1969 by Children of the Day.
2. Peterson, *A Long Obedience in the Same Direction*, p. 136.
3. *The New Bible Commentary*, ed. Guthrie, p. 506.
4. Spurgeon, *The Treasury of David*, Vol. II, Psalm 107, p. 402.

## Part Three
## The Essentials
## of Intimacy

**Reverence for God**

**Truthfulness with God**

**Love for God's Word**

---

God is a willing and worthy confidant. But to know Him and enjoy Him as confidant involves certain responses on our part.

Fellowship with the Creator demands our respect and reverence of Him as majestic and holy. In *The Practice of Godliness*, Jerry Bridges writes, "The fear of God is a heartfelt recognition of the gap between God the Creator and man the creature" (NavPress, p. 29). Reverence for God is essential in maintaining our proper relationship with Him.

This reverence frees us to be totally vulnerable and honest before God, because as our Creator He knows us fully. The psalmists, confident in God's knowledge of them, are refreshingly truthful. Kidner observes of these honest prayers, "The very presence of such prayers in Scripture is a witness to His understanding. He knows how men speak when they are desperate" (*Tyndale O. T. Commentaries: Psalms 1-72*, gen.

ed. D. J. Wiseman: InterVarsity Press, 1973, p. 157).

Psalm 119, the longest psalm, is a glowing tribute to another essential element of intimacy with God: desire for God's Word. The writer of this psalm had a passion for God and His Word, and his intimacy with God is very evident. One of the major ways of deepening our relationship with our Lord is to know and love His Word.

These next three chapters are important, because they speak of our responsibility in developing intimacy. In them we learn what we can do to progressively discover the God who will never allow the righteous to be shaken!

## CHAPTER SEVEN
## Reverence for God

———————◆———————

Friendship with God is reserved for those
who reverence him.
With them alone he shares the secrets of his promises.
(Psalm 25:14, TLB)

◆

O worship the King all glorious above,
And gratefully sing His wonderful love;
Our Shield and Defender, the Ancient of Days,
Pavilioned in splendor and girded with praise.[1]

◆

While we must never on the one hand lose the freedom to
enter boldly and joyfully by faith into God's presence
during our lives on earth, we must also learn how to
revere God in our relationship with Him . . .
intimacy cannot occur without respect.[2]
(John White)

| Words/phrases that describe God's character | Corresponding implications for a life that reverences God | vv. |
| --- | --- | --- |
| Psalm 15 | | |
| Psalm 24 | | |
| Psalm 34 | | |
| Psalm 111 | | |
| Psalm 112

(Skip this column for Psalm 112) | | |

# Reverence for God

A. F. Kirkpatrick has written, "Fear and love are the insepara-
ble elements of true religion. Fear preserves love from
degenerating into presumptuous familiarity; love prevents
fear from becoming a servile and cringing dread."[3] True
intimacy with God involves not only our love for Him, but
also our reverence and respect. The psalmists speak often of
fearing God, and of the great blessings bestowed on those
who do. Throughout the psalms we are reminded that by His
very nature, God commands our reverence, respect, awe, and
fear.

> For great is the LORD, and greatly to be praised;
> He is to be feared above all gods.
> For all the gods of the peoples are idols,
> But the LORD made the heavens.
> Splendor and majesty are before Him,
> Strength and beauty are in His sanctuary.
>
> Psalm 96:4-6

## Observation

1. The passages in this chapter speak of the psalmists' recognition of God's holy character and the importance of fearing God. Using the chart on page 52, write down the words
   or phrases the psalmist uses to describe God's character.
   Then write down what the psalmist identifies as the corresponding implications for a life that demonstrates reverence for God.

"Fears the Lord." *Reverence* might be a better word. Awe. The
Bible isn't interested in whether we believe in God or not. It
assumes that everyone more or less does. What it is interested
in is the response we have toward him: Will we let God be as he
is, majestic and holy, vast and wondrous, or will we always be

53

trying to whittle him down to the size of our small minds, insist on confining him within the boundaries we are comfortable with, refuse to think of him other than in images that are convenient to our lifestyle?[4]

Eugene Peterson

## Reflection

2. Look back through the passages you observed in question 1 of this lesson. What blessings accompany a life that fears God? (For additional passages, note Psalms 25:14 and 145:19, quoted in this lesson.)

3. Why would these implications for a life that demonstrates reverence for God necessarily follow or correspond to a recognition of God's holy character?

4. The life described by the psalmists in these passages may seem difficult to attain. How do God's responses to those who fear Him encourage us to live this kind of life?

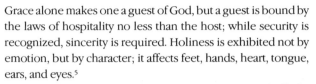

Grace alone makes one a guest of God, but a guest is bound by the laws of hospitality no less than the host; while security is recognized, sincerity is required. Holiness is exhibited not by emotion, but by character; it affects feet, hands, heart, tongue, ears, and eyes.[5]

A. G. Clarke

## Expression

After studying these psalms, I am challenged to examine my life in terms of how it reflects reverence for God. For example, Psalm 24:4 brought to mind my tendency to try to please people. I find myself at times "lifting my soul to falsehood," or compromising the truth, in an effort to spare someone's feelings or make another think well of me. I have asked the Lord to show me immediately when I do this. He is very faithful to make me aware of my sin and to help me realize that by doing this, I am not reverencing His name. This prayer has also been helpful: "I am lying; Lord, increase my abhorrence of it. I would endeavor to cleanse myself from all filthiness: there will never be a mortified tongue while there is an unmortified heart."[6]

5. In light of this chapter, what specific application could you begin to make that would enable your life to more vividly demonstrate reverence and respect for the Lord?

Robert Nisbet writes concerning the fear of God: "It is the fear which a child feels toward an honored parent—a fear to offend; it is that which they who have been rescued from destruction feel to the benefactor who nobly and at the sacrifice interposed for their safety—a fear to act unworthily of his kindness: it is that which fills the breast of a pardoned and grateful rebel in the presence of a venerated sovereign at whose throne he is permitted to stand in honor—a fear lest he should ever forget his goodness and give him cause to regret it. Such is the fear of the Christian now: a fear which reverence for majesty, gratitude for mercies, dread of displeasure, desire of approval, and longing for the fellowship of heaven, inspire."[7]

He fulfills the desires of those who fear him;
he hears their cry and saves them.
Psalm 145:19, NIV

**Other Scriptures:** Proverbs 3:7-8, 2 Corinthians 5:10-11

**Notes**

1. From the hymn "O Worship the King," by Robert Grant, adapted from Johann M. Haydn.
2. John White, *Daring to Draw Near* (Downers Grove, IL: InterVarsity Press, 1977), pp. 99-100.
3. A. F. Kirkpatrick, *The Book of Psalms* (Grand Rapids: Baker Book House, 1982), p. 817.
4. Peterson, *A Long Obedience in the Same Direction*, p. 116.
5. A. G. Clarke, *Analytical Studies in the Psalms* (Grand Rapids: Kregel Publications, 1979), p. 61.
6. Benjamin Bennett, "A Christian Oratory," in *Psalms*, by Charles Haddon Spurgeon, ed. David Otis Fuller (Grand Rapids: Kregel Publications, 1968), p. 62.
7. Robert Nisbet, in *Psalms*, by Spurgeon, ed. Fuller, p. 594.

## CHAPTER EIGHT
## Truthfulness with God

---◆---

Lord, all my desire is before Thee;
And my sighing is not hidden from Thee.
(Psalm 38:9)

◆

Tempted and tried, I need a great Savior,
One who can help my burdens to bear;
I must tell Jesus, I must tell Jesus,
He all my cares and sorrows will share.[1]

◆

David emphasized two aspects of prayer: honesty before
God, and the fear of God. To "call upon him in truth" simply
means "to call on him sincerely." If we want to have revival
in our lives, we must begin by being totally honest with God
in our praying. But we must not allow this "honesty" to
degenerate into undue familiarity; we must "fear him" and
show the proper respect and reverence.[2]
(Warren Wiersbe)

| David's requests | vv. |
|---|---|
| Psalm 25 | |
| Psalm 39 | |
| Psalm 51 | |
| Psalm 109 | |
| Psalm 142 | |

# Truthfulness with God

I once read a greeting card with the following thoughts written on the front: "Let us live, let us love, let us share the deepest secrets of our souls. . . ." The inside of the card read, "You go first."

How true is this impulse in developing intimacy! We don't want to be the first to bare our souls. God, however, has gone first in our relationship with Him. He initiates, He calls, He sends, He provides, He gives—all for us to know Him, to draw near to Him. Once we know and experience God as righteous, trustworthy, responsive, and our refuge, we can begin to feel comfortable with sharing our deepest secrets. David, vulnerable and honest, shows us as no other that it is permissible—even desirable—to "drop our guard" in communing with God.

> You know my folly, O God;
> my guilt is not hidden from you.
>
> Psalm 69:5, NIV

## Observation

1. In simplicity and deep sincerity, David prayed and sang fervently to God. As you read the psalms listed in the chart on the preceding page, make note of the requests David asks of God on his own behalf.

--------◆--------

God's love accepts us without reserve. What is acceptance? A writer in *Eternity* magazine [October 1969] gives the following analysis: "Acceptance means you are valuable just as you are. It allows you to be the real you. You aren't forced into someone else's idea of who you really are. It means your ideas are taken seriously since they reflect you. You can talk about how you feel inside and why you feel that way, and someone really cares. Acceptance means you can try out your ideas without being

shot down. You can even express heretical thoughts and dis-
cuss them with intelligent questioning. You feel safe. No one
will pronounce judgment on you even though they don't agree
with you. It doesn't mean you will never be corrected or shown
to be wrong; it simply means it's safe to be you and no one will
destroy you out of prejudice."[3]

---◆---

### Reflection

2. Review the requests David made. What basic aspects of his
life does he share with God?




3. In these psalms, what words or phrases denote David's
vulnerability before God?




4. As David wrote these psalms, he mentioned various facets
of God's character and responses to His people. List some
of these truths about God that enabled David to be honest
with Him.

The committing of our cause to God is at once our duty, our safety, and our ease.[4]

Abraham Wright

## Expression

Over and over again in my life, I find myself pulled, pressured, and perplexed. As I sort through all my options, I am finally reduced to one basic cry: "Well, Lord, it really is just You and me, isn't it?" Over and over again, God patiently, but piercingly, replies, "Yes, Cynthia, it's true. But am I *enough* for you?" I, then, must say with David: "I cry to thee, O LORD, and say, 'Thou art my refuge; thou art all I have in the land of the living'" (Psalm 142:5, NEB).

5. Is there some aspect of your life you struggle to bring before God? Or some questions, feelings, or reflections—positive or negative—you long to be able to tell Him? Using these psalms as examples, write a brief prayer or psalm expressing how you feel about these concerns.

We do not pray to tell God what he does not know, nor to remind him of things he has forgotten. He already cares for the things we pray about; his attention to them has never flagged from the beginning, and his understanding is unfathomable. He has simply been waiting for us to care about them with him.[5]

Tim Stafford

**Other Scriptures:** Jeremiah 20:7-18, Luke 22:39-44

**Notes**
1. From the hymn "I Must Tell Jesus," by Elisha A. Hoffman.
2. Warren Wiersbe, *Meet Yourself in the Psalms* (Wheaton, IL: Victor Books, 1983), p. 21.
3. Ray Stedman, *Folk Songs of Faith*, from the *Bible Commentary for Laymen* series, p. 274.
4. Abraham Wright, in *Psalms*, by Spurgeon, ed. Fuller, p. 654.
5. Tim Stafford, *Knowing the Face of God* (Grand Rapids: Zondervan Books, 1986), p. 134.

## CHAPTER NINE
## Love for God's Word

◆

The judgments of the LORD are true;
they are righteous altogether.
They are more desirable than gold,
yes, than much fine gold;
Sweeter also than honey
and the drippings of the honeycomb.
(Psalm 19:9-10)

◆

How firm a foundation, ye saints of the Lord,
Is laid for your faith in His excellent Word!
What more can He say than to you He hath said,
To you who for refuge to Jesus have fled?[1]

◆

Heart-fellowship with God is enjoyed through a love
of the Word, which is God's way of
communing with the soul by His Spirit.[2]
(C. H. Spurgeon)

# Love for God's Word

The "Psalm of the Saints," "The Alphabet of Divine Love," "The Christian's Golden A-B-C of the Praise, Love, Power, and Use of the Word of God" are some of the titles and descriptions given to Psalm 119.

Three major guidelines were used by the writer of this impressive psalm. The first was to address God continually (only four verses do not), the second is to extol the Word of God (only two verses do not mention the Scriptures), and the third guideline was to make the psalm an acrostic by using the letters of the Hebrew alphabet to begin each section and verse.

Charles Spurgeon notes that "this sacred ode is a little Bible, the Scriptures condensed, a mass of Bibline, Holy Writ rewritten in holy emotions and actions. . . . Oh, that every reader may feel the glow which is poured over the verses as they proceed: he will then begin as a reader, but he will soon bow as a suppliant; his study will become an oratory, and his contemplation will warm into adoration."[3]

May we say with the psalmist:

> I wait for the LORD, my soul does wait,
> And in His word do I hope.
>
> Psalm 130:5

## Observation

1. Spurgeon writes concerning Psalm 119: "Nor is it long only; for it equally excells in breadth of thought, depth of meaning, and height of fervor."[4] This psalm is indeed rich! As you read carefully through the psalm, record your observations under the proper headings given below. You do not have to write down *every* prayer, key phrase, or ministry of the Word you find; only write down the thoughts, words, verses that are especially meaningful to you.

a. Write down the various synonyms used for the Word of God.

b. Record the functions or ministry of the Word to the psalmist.

c. What were some of the specific prayers or petitions of the psalmist?

d. What key words or phrases did the psalmist use to communicate his love for the law?

---◆---

The whole Psalm is animated by a profound inwardness and spirituality, as far removed as possible from the superstitious literalism of a later age. It shows no tendency to substitute mechanical observance of rules for the living application of principles. The close personal relation of the Psalmist to God is one of the most striking features of the Psalms in general, and in few Psalms is it more marked than in this.[5]

A. F. Kirkpatrick

---◆---

## Reflection

2. Write a brief paragraph summarizing why you think the psalmist loved and delighted in the Word of God.

———————◆———————

I know of no part of the Holy Scriptures where the nature and evidence of true and sincere godliness are so fully and largely insisted on and delineated as in the One Hundred Nineteenth Psalm.[6]

Jonathan Edwards

———————◆———————

## Expression

One of the amazing characteristics of this psalm is that it is a perfect acrostic. The psalmist has taken the twenty-two letters of the Hebrew alphabet and divided the psalm into twenty-two sections with each section representing a different letter of the alphabet. Then, each of the verses in each section begins with that same letter. Several psalms are acrostics and the psalmists wrote this way to aid their memory. Not only is this psalm unique in its focus and devotion to God and His Word; it is an amazing example of the author's commitment to detail.

3. Below is my effort at expressing my thoughts using a letter of the alphabet. Take time to express your desire for God's Word using one or two letters of the alphabet.

All of Your words are true, Lord;
    help me to live by them.
Arouse my heart to love the Scriptures
    so that I will obey them.
Anoint me with Your Spirit
    that I may understand Your way.

---

In Matthew Henry's "Account of the Life and Death of His Father, Philip Henry," he says: "Once, pressing the study of the Scriptures, he advised us to take a verse of the Psalm [119] every morning to meditate upon, and so go over the Psalm twice in the year; and that, saith he, will bring you to be in love with all the rest of the Scriptures. He often said, 'All grace grows as love for the Word of God grows.'"[7]

---

**Other Scriptures:** Deuteronomy 30:8-14, Colossians 3:16

### Notes
1. From the hymn "How Firm a Foundation."
2. Spurgeon, *Psalms*, ed. Fuller, p. 511.
3. Spurgeon, *Psalms*, ed. Fuller, pp. 510-511.
4. Spurgeon, *Psalms*, ed. Fuller, p. 519.
5. Kirkpatrick, *The Book of Psalms*, p. 701.
6. Jonathan Edwards, in *Psalms*, by Spurgeon, ed. Fuller, p. 511.
7. Spurgeon, *Psalms*, ed. Fuller, p. 510.

Part Four
# The Fruit of Intimacy

---

### The Growth of Intimacy
### Praise: The Expression of Intimacy
### Deepening Our Intimacy with God

---

◆

---

True intimacy with God leaves us with a desire for deeper intimacy. The more we know our God, the more we want to know Him. The Creator becomes our confidant, and that is enough. Our thoughts and our voices are lifted in prayer and praise to God and God alone—beautiful evidences of the fruit of intimacy.

# CHAPTER TEN
## The Growth of Intimacy

———◆———

Because he has loved Me, therefore I will deliver him;
I will set him securely on high,
because he has known My name.
(Psalm 91:14)

◆

When peace, like a river, attendeth my way,
When sorrows like sea billows roll—
Whatever my lot, Thou hast taught me to say,
It is well, it is well with my soul.[1]

◆

To have found God, to have experienced Him in the
intimacy of our beings, to have lived even for one hour in
the fire of His Trinity and the bliss of His unity clearly makes
us say: "Now I understand. You alone are enough for me."[2]
(Carlo Corretto)

| Responses to God | Responses to others | Personal growth | vv. |
|---|---|---|---|
| Psalm 16 | | | |
| Psalm 26 | | | |
| Psalm 27 | | | |
| Psalm 55 | | | |
| Psalm 100 | | | |
| Psalm 131 | | | |

# The Growth of Intimacy

A young girl was asked to recite Psalm 23 in her Sunday school class. She began by saying, "The Lord is my shepherd; He is all I want." One who is growing in intimacy with God would paraphrase this passage from Psalm 23 in the same way. As we mature in our Christian life, we can begin to say, "Whatever my lot—it is well with my soul." The psalms in this chapter beautifully record the difference that the psalmists' intimate relationship with God made in their lives. What is true for the psalmists can also be true for us.

> What shall I render to the LORD
> For all His benefits toward me?
> I shall lift up the cup of salvation,
> And call upon the name of the LORD.
> I shall pay my vows to the LORD,
> Oh may it be in the presence of all His people.
> Psalm 116:12-14

## Observation

1. One who is intimate with God begins to experience changes in thoughts, attitudes, and responses to God and life. As you read the psalms listed on page 74, record the responses the psalmists had to God, to others, and the personal growth they experienced as a result of their intimacy with Him. (Some psalms will not need all columns.)

---◆---

> Holiness is a behavior as well as a belief. It isn't the difference between "criminal" and "law-abiding." It is the difference between good and best. We practice holiness because of friendship with God. There is no semifriendship, no occasional fear of the Lord.[3]
>
> Roger Palms

---◆---

## Reflection

2. What evidences of the psalmist's intimacy with God can you find in these passages?

3. Summarize the key changes found in the psalmist's life as a result of his intimacy with God.

————————◆————————

Once the joy of intimacy with God has been experienced, life becomes unbearable without it.[4]

J. O. Sanders

————————◆————————

## Expression

These psalms have been very meaningful to me. David especially expresses so vividly his deep and intimate relationship with God. My life is more than half over and I have only begun to know God, to develop even a surface relationship with Him. Perhaps, though, this is the essence of intimacy: not being satisfied or complacent, but always desiring to go deeper into the fullness of God.

4. Which of these psalms or verses could you identify with the most? Why are these verses important to you?

---◆---

I do not seek, O Lord, to penetrate Thy depths. I by no means think my intellect equal to them: but I long to understand in some degree Thy truth, which my heart believes and loves. For I do not seek to understand that I may believe; but I believe that I may understand.[5]

Saint Anselm

---◆---

**Other Scriptures:** Exodus 33:7-23, John 15:1-17

**Notes**

1. From the hymn "It Is Well with My Soul," by Horatio G. Spafford and Philip P. Bliss.
2. Carlo Corretto, in *A Guide to Prayer for Ministers and Other Servants*, by Reuben P. Job and Norman Sawchuck (Nashville, TN: Upper Room Publishers, 1983), p. 15.
3. Roger C. Palms, *The Pleasure of His Company: How to Be a Friend of God* (Wheaton, IL: Tyndale House Publishers, 1982), p. 57.
4. Sanders, *Enjoying Intimacy With God*, p. 66.
5. "Prayer of Anselm," in *Psalms*, by Spurgeon, ed. Fuller, p. 605.

## CHAPTER ELEVEN
## Praise: The Expression of Intimacy

---

I will sing to the LORD as long as I live;
I will sing praise to my God while I have my being.
(Psalm 104:33)

◆

O for a thousand tongues to sing
My great Redeemer's praise,
The glories of my God and King,
The triumphs of His grace![1]

◆

Don't underestimate the value of praise.
There is something about expressing your appreciation to
God in words, song, and meditation that solidifies your faith.
The Book of Psalms is the Bible's hymnal of praise. The
more you praise God for being who He is—a loving God
who judges righteously—the more you can act upon your
belief of what He is—eternal love.[2]
(Josh McDowell)

| Why is God to be praised? | Who is to praise God? | vv. |
|---|---|---|
| Psalm 67 | | |
| Psalm 95 | | |
| Psalm 96 | | |
| Psalm 148 | | |
| Psalm 150 | | |

# Praise: The Expression of Intimacy

Charles Spurgeon has written, "Praise should be proportionate to its object; therefore let it be infinite when rendered unto the Lord. We cannot praise Him too much, too often, too zealously, too carefully, too joyfully."[3] The psalms do teach us to praise God much, often, zealously, and joyfully. When our praise seems so inadequate, how encouraging to turn to the psalms and find the freedom and joy of these hymns to God. It is exciting to begin to exalt God by awakening the dawn with the harp, lyre, and songs of praises to His holy name!

> Awake, my glory;
> Awake, harp and lyre,
> I will awaken the dawn!
> I will give thanks to Thee, O Lord, among the peoples;
> I will sing praises to Thee among the nations.
>
> Psalm 57:8-9

## Observation

1. Praise is essential to worshiping God and to relating to Him. The psalms guide us specifically in how to praise God. Look for reasons why God is to be praised and for guidelines on who is to praise Him, as you read the psalms listed in the chart on page 80.

---◆---

> The highest praise of God is to declare what He is. We can invent nothing which would magnify the Lord: we can never extol Him better than by repeating His name or describing His character. The Lord is to be extolled as creating all things that exist and as doing so by the simple agency of His Word. He created by a command; what a power is this![4]
>
> C. H. Spurgeon

---◆---

## Reflection

2. The psalmists both command and invite us to praise. What do you think motivated the psalmists to encourage praise so strongly?

3. The Hebrew title for the book of Psalms is "book of praises." Many of the psalms were written to be sung as hymns of praise for God's character and deeds. What benefits do you think the people might have gained from singing these remembrances of God's faithfulness to them?

———————◆———————

Some Christians praise the Lord and some do not. Perhaps the difference is this: the believers who praise the Lord have their eyes of faith fixed on Him, while the silent saints look only at themselves. When God is the center of your life, you can praise Him every day, because you will always find blessings no matter how difficult your circumstances. To a praising saint, the circumstances of life are a window through which he sees God. To a complaining saint, these same circumstances are only a mirror in which he sees himself. That is why he complains.[5]

Warren Wiersbe

———————◆———————

## Expression

Praising God is not natural to me. Studying praise in the Scriptures has challenged me to increase my praise life and to be more aware of the Creator and His creation. There has been only one time in my life when I have been deeply moved to write a praise to God. Our plane had been circling the Denver airport for thirty minutes. Tired and frustrated, I kept staring at the thick cloud cover that was responsible for our delay. As the plane turned, I was startled to see the most beautiful oranges, yellows, and pinks brilliantly scrolled across the sky. Tears sprang to my eyes. I guess that I had never witnessed a sunset from 30,000 feet! I was so deeply moved by this bold reminder from God that the following thought resulted:

> Etched into the sunset,
> the signature of God.
> In radiant script
> He signs
> I AM.

4. Begin to think about how you can increase your praise and personal worship of the Lord. For example:

   * Include a favorite hymn or song of praise in your devotional times.
   * Use one of the psalms in this chapter, or another of your choosing, as a guide for offering praises to God.
   * Look for opportunities in your daily routine to praise God. Consider recording these thoughts in a journal or notebook for later reflection.

Charles Spurgeon writes concerning Psalm 150: "Once more, 'Hallelujah!' Thus is the Psalm rounded with a note of praise, and thus is the Book of Psalms ended by a glowing word of adoration. Reader, wilt not thou at this moment pause a while and worship the Lord, thy God? *Hallelujah!*"[6]

**Other Scriptures:** 1 Chronicles 29:10-13, Ephesians 5:18-20, Hebrews 13:15, Revelation 4:1-11

### Notes

1. From the hymn "O for a Thousand Tongues to Sing," by Charles Wesley and Carl G. Gläser.
2. Josh McDowell and Dale Bellis, *Evidence for Joy* (Waco, TX: Word Books, 1984), pp. 107-108.
3. Spurgeon, *Psalms*, ed. Fuller, p. 404.
4. Spurgeon, *Psalms*, ed. Fuller, p. 681.
5. Wiersbe, *Meet Yourself in the Psalms*, pp. 12-13.
6. Spurgeon, *Psalms*, ed. Fuller, p. 687.

## CHAPTER TWELVE
## Deepening Our Intimacy with God

---◆---

O come, let us sing for joy to the LORD;
Let us shout joyfully to the rock of our salvation.
Let us come before His presence with thanksgiving;
Let us shout joyfully to Him with psalms.
(Psalm 95:1-2)

◆

Once earthly joy I craved, Sought peace and rest;
Now Thee alone I seek, Give what is best;
This all my prayer shall be: More love, O Christ, to Thee,
More love to Thee, more love to Thee![1]

◆

It would seem that admission to the inner circle of
deepening intimacy with God is the outcome of *deep desire*.
Only those who count such intimacy a prize worth sacrific-
ing anything else for, are likely to attain it. If other intimacies
are more desirable to us, we will not gain entry to that circle.

The place on Jesus' breast is still vacant, and open to any
who are willing to pay the price of deepening intimacy. We
are now, and we will be in the future, only as intimate with
God as we really choose to be.[2]
(J. O. Sanders)

| Aspects of intimacy | vv. |
|---|---|
| Psalm 7 | |
| Psalm 57 | |
| Psalm 146 | |

# Deepening Our Intimacy with God

I watched the flight attendant pull the curtain that separated the first-class passengers on the plane from those of us flying coach class.

That curtain reminded me of the veil used to set apart the Holy of Holies in the Hebrew temple. There were strict rules regarding who was allowed to enter and when, for the Holy of Holies represented intimacy with God.

This temple veil was dramatically torn from top to bottom when Jesus spoke from the cross with His last breath, "It is finished." Now, through Christ, there is immediate access: the privilege and opportunity of intimacy with God is ours at any time.

And yet, as Sanders has stated, we are only as close to Jesus as we choose to be. The goal of this chapter is to encourage our continuing intimacy with the Lord.

> How blessed is the man who does not walk in
> the counsel of the wicked,
> Nor stand in the path of sinners,
> Nor sit in the seat of scoffers!
> But his delight is in the law of the LORD,
> And in His law he meditates day and night.
> Psalm 1:1-2

## Observation

1. a. This Bible study has explored many elements of intimacy: the desire for intimacy—our longing for God, His desire for us—God as our confidant, the essentials of intimacy, and the fruit of intimacy.

   As you read the psalms in the chart on page 86, record whatever aspects of intimacy you find expressed by the psalmists.

b. Now choose your favorite psalm, either from this study or one you have not yet studied, and record the different aspects of intimacy you find in it.

---◆---

God wants you near him and wants lovingly to guide your life. There is still that one clear certainty in an age when nothing else is certain at all: God wants you to be his friend. He wants to give you the pleasure of his company.[3]

Roger Palms

---◆---

**Reflection**

2. Which chapter in this study has helped you the most in deepening your intimacy with God? Why?

3. Take some time now to reflect on your understanding or experience of intimacy as it has developed through this

study. (You may want to flip back through the pages to some of your more significant insights or discoveries.) What major lesson have you learned concerning your relationship with God? How can this insight affect your future growth in the Lord?

———————◆———————

I want deliberately to encourage this mighty longing after God. The lack of it has brought us to our present low estate. The stiff and wooden quality about our religious lives is a result of our lack of holy desire. Complacency is a deadly foe of all spiritual growth. Acute desire must be present or there will be no manifestation of Christ to His people. He waits to be wanted. Too bad that with many of us He waits so long, so very long, in vain.[4]

A. W. Tozer

———————◆———————

## Expression

C. Donald Cole has observed, "David was in earnest about praying, so much so that he wrote out his prayers after he had made them."[5] What a good idea! Perhaps you would like to start writing your own psalms, prayers, or paragraphs to God. Begin to keep a spiritual journal of your feelings for the Lord, for others, for yourself. Continue to read through the psalms and study different topics and themes found in these scriptures. Choose parts or whole psalms to memorize, so that your meditation will be rich and meaningful. As this discipline becomes a part of your life, how exciting it will be to look back and realize a growing intimacy with the Creator, who has become your confidant!

> Thy Spirit
>> quickening my spirit.
> Thy thoughts
>> renewing mine.
> My will
>> yielding to Thy will.
> My heart
>> becoming as Thine.

4. Ronald Klug provides this helpful guidance for starting a spiritual journal: "There are no rules for keeping a spiritual journal. Your way is the right way."[6] Write out your own sample journal entry by choosing one of the following ideas:

* Rephrase your answer to question 3 of this chapter in the form of a prayer or psalm to God.
* Select a favorite psalm—perhaps the one you chose in question 1b of this chapter—and write out a prayer or paragraph telling the Lord what this psalm means to you and why.
* Choose an especially significant insight, reflection, or application that came up during your study of the psalms and write out two or three paragraphs describing it and why it was significant.

"The end of a matter," wrote Solomon, "is better than its beginning."[7] But the end of this study guide can actually be the beginning of a deepening experience of intimacy with God, if that is your desire. The psalmists have taught us so much about our need for intimacy and how God desires to fulfill that need continually in our lives. Because of God's faithfulness and the testimonies of the psalmists, we, too, can begin to experience the joy of intimacy.

———————◆———————

O Lord my God! when I in awesome wonder
Consider all the worlds Thy hands have made,
I see the stars, I hear the rolling thunder,
Thy power throughout the universe displayed:

Then sings my soul, my Savior God, to Thee;
How great Thou art, how great Thou art!
Then sings my soul, my Savior God, to Thee;
How great Thou art, how great Thou art![8]

———————◆———————

### Notes

1. From the hymn "More Love to Thee, O Christ," by William H. Doane and Elizabeth P. Prentiss.
2. Sanders, *Enjoying Intimacy with God*, p. 20.
3. Palms, *The Pleasure of His Company: How to Be a Friend of God*, p. 66.
4. Tozer, *The Pursuit of God*, p. 17.
5. C. Donald Cole, *Thirsting for God* (Westchester, IL: Crossway Books, 1986), p. 298.
6. Ronald Klug, *How to Keep a Spiritual Journal* (Nashville, TN: Thomas Nelson Publishers, 1982), p. 58.
7. Ecclesiastes 7:8.
8. From the hymn "How Great Thou Art," by Stuart K. Hine.

# SUGGESTIONS FOR FURTHER STUDY
## IN THE PSALMS

The psalms are so rich that you may want to continue your study of them in different areas. Here are some suggestions for further study topics in the book of Psalms:

* The names of God.
* The attributes of God.
* Metaphors for God.
* God's desire for His people.
* Christ in the psalms.
* Prophecy in the psalms.
* David's circumstances/historical background behind the psalms—for example, Psalms 55 and 88 (you will need to go outside the Psalms for this subject, to the Old Testament history books and also to some reference works).

You might also want to consider going back through this study, or selected chapters of it, using psalms of your own choosing or ones in the chapters you might not have had enough time to go through thoroughly.

### Suggested reference works on the Psalms:

A. G. Clarke. *Analytical Studies in the Psalms.* Grand Rapids: Kregel Publications, 1979.

C. Donald Cole, *Thirsting for God.* Westchester, IL: Crossway Books, 1986.

A. F. Kirkpatrick. *The Book of Psalms.* Grand Rapids: Baker Book House, 1982.

Charles Haddon Spurgeon. *Psalms.* Ed. David Otis Fuller. Grand Rapids: Kregel Publications, 1968.

Charles Haddon Spurgeon. *The Treasury of David* (3 vols.). MacLean, VA: MacDonald Publishing Co., n.d.

Bible commentaries and encyclopedias.

# YOU CAN LEAD DYNAMIC, LIFE-CHANGING SMALL-GROUP BIBLE STUDIES!

We hope you've enjoyed this NavPress study guide. Good materials are only part of what makes a successful and fulfilling small-group experience. That's why NavPress is pleased to announce PILGRIMAGE/NAVPRESS SMALL-GROUP TRAINING SEMINARS.

Whether you've led groups for years or are just starting out, PILGRIMAGE/NAVPRESS SMALL GROUP TRAINING will help you create and lead the kind of groups that foster life-changing spiritual growth.

In just 7 hours you'll learn:

▶ "Hands-on" small-group training techniques from the leading experts in North America

▶ The 7 essential skills every effective small-group leader needs

▶ How groups can specialize in worship, evangelism, discipleship, and emotional healing

▶ How small groups can help entire church bodies increase in love for one another

PILGRIMAGE/NAVPRESS SMALL-GROUP TRAINING SEMINARS are held at hundreds of locations all over North America. Call 1-800-GRPS-R-US for more information about seminars available in your area.

## 1-800-477-7787

PILGRIMAGE
NAVPRESS

# SMALL-GROUP MATERIALS FROM NAVPRESS

## BIBLE STUDY SERIES

DESIGN FOR DISCIPLESHIP
GOD IN YOU
GOD'S DESIGN FOR THE FAMILY
INSTITUTE OF BIBLICAL
   COUNSELING Series
LEARNING TO LOVE Series

LIFECHANGE
RADICAL RELATIONSHIPS
SPIRITUAL DISCIPLINES
STUDIES IN CHRISTIAN LIVING
THINKING THROUGH DISCIPLESHIP

## TOPICAL BIBLE STUDIES

Becoming a Woman of Excellence
Becoming a Woman of Freedom
Becoming a Woman of Prayer
Becoming a Woman of Purpose
The Blessing Study Guide
Homemaking
Intimacy with God
Loving Your Husband

Loving Your Wife
A Mother's Legacy
Praying From God's Heart
Surviving Life in the Fast Lane
To Run and Not Grow Tired
To Walk and Not Grow Weary
What God Does When Men Pray
When the Squeeze Is On

## BIBLE STUDIES WITH COMPANION BOOKS

Bold Love
Daughters of Eve
The Discipline of Grace
The Feminine Journey
Inside Out
The Masculine Journey
The Practice of Godliness
The Pursuit of Holiness

Secret Longings of the Heart
Spiritual Disciplines
Tame Your Fears
Transforming Grace
Trusting God
What Makes a Man?
The Wounded Heart

## RESOURCES

Brothers!
Discipleship Journal's Best
   Small-Group Ideas
How to Build a Small Groups Ministry
How to Lead Small Groups
Jesus Cares for Women
The Navigator Bible Studies
   Handbook

The Small Group Leaders
   Training Course
Topical Memory System
   (KJV/NIV and NASB/NKJV)
Topical Memory System:
   Life Issues

If you liked *Intimacy with God,* look for these other studies by Cynthia Heald:

# THE ONLY BIBLE STUDY ON THE TOP-TEN BESTSELLER LIST.

Society beckons us to succeed—to achieve excellence in our appearance, our earning power, our family life. God Himself beckons us to be women of excellence.

But what exactly is He asking?

Striking at the heart of what the Bible has to say about becoming a godly woman, these eleven lessons will help you understand what excellence means in such areas as:

- Surrender • Obedience • Discipline • Discretion
- Wisdom • Purity • A gentle and quiet spirit

Cynthia's personal reflections as well as quotes from Christian thinkers make each lesson fresh and relevant. Challenging questions will help you "approve the things that are excellent" and experience the joy of becoming God's woman of excellence.

***Becoming a Woman of Excellence***
by Cynthia Heald  (Paperback; ISBN 0891090665)

# RUN THE RACE WITH FREEDOM.

If you ever feel that you're making no progress, lacking joy, or being weighed down in your Christian life—in spite of all you're doing to grow and serve— *Becoming a Woman of Freedom* will give you a second wind.

In this spirit-lifting study, Cynthia Heald will help you identify and lay aside the burdens that can make you feel "stuck," including:

- Past hurt and loss • Poor self-image • Approval seeking
- Busyness • Doubt and fear • Unhealthy influences

With challenging insights and thought-provoking quotations from classic thinkers and writers, *Becoming a Woman of Freedom* will put you on the road to freedom—and help you develop the actions and attitudes you'll need to finish the race with strength.

***Becoming a Woman of Freedom*** by Cynthia Heald  (Paperback; ISBN 0891096752)

# TWELVE WAYS TO BUILD YOUR MARRIAGE.

How can you be the woman and wife God designed you to be in the context of an imperfect world? In this Bible study, Cynthia Heald will encourage you in the lifelong process of discovering these things. As she leads you through key Scripture passages, you'll learn 12 ways to apply biblical truth to the personal joys and struggles of your own marriage.

***Loving Your Husband: Building an Intimate Marriage in a Fallen World***
by Cynthia Heald  (Paperback; ISBN 0891095446)

• • • •

Marriage in an imperfect world can seem disappointing at times. In *Loving Your Wife,* you'll explore twelve things you can do to strengthen and improve your marriage, including how to cultivate a compassionate, self-sacrificing, forgiving spirit toward your wife; discern and meet her needs; and adopt a leadership style that will foster intimacy, confidence, and respect.

***Loving Your Wife: Building an Intimate Marriage in a Fallen World***
by Jack and Cynthia Heald  (Paperback; ISBN 0891095756)

**These and other NavPress Bible studies are available
at your local Christian bookstore.  Or call 1-800-366-7788.**

## NAVPRESS ◑
### BRINGING TRUTH TO LIFE